ETAL CAST

NORTHUMBERLAND

Ian S Nelson

The remains of Etal Castle dominate the picturesque village of Etal. The castle was built in the early fourteenth century by Robert Manners, in a strategic position by a ford over the River Till. As a border stronghold, Etal was vulnerable to attack from Scottish raiders, and in 1341 Robert was granted a licence to fortify his home, adding curtain walls, corner towers and a gatehouse. In 1513, Etal was suddenly thrust into the forefront of national events, as it was captured by the Scots during James IV's attempted invasion of England. The Scots were subsequently defeated at the Battle of Flodden, and Etal was freed. The union of the English and Scottish crowns in 1603 ended the castle's active role in history, and it fell into a state of disrepair. It was eventually abandoned in the eighteenth century, and the owners moved to a more comfortable manor house at the other end of the village. Etal was sold at the turn of the century to the Joicey family, who have done much to restore the castle and village. This guidebook provides a tour around the remains of the castle, followed by a history of the site and its owners.

❖ CONTENTS ❖

Published by English Heritage
23 Savile Row, London W1S 2ET
Copyright © English Heritage 1998
First published by English Heritage 1998, reprinted 2001

Photographs by English Heritage Photographic Unit
and copyright of English Heritage, unless otherwise stated.

Edited by Susannah Lawson
Designed by Pauline Hull
Printed in England by Sterling Press
C30, 7/01, FA1969, ISBN 1-85074-699-0

DESCRIPTION
AND TOUR

❖

ETAL CASTLE today is but a
shadow of its former self, con-
sisting of a tower house, a gatehouse
and a length of curtain wall which
connects the gatehouse with the
remains of a third tower beside the
custodian's house. There is likely to
have been a fourth tower in the
north-east corner of the courtyard,
linked to the other parts of the castle
by curtain walls. In the centre was a
courtyard in which there were a
number of ancillary buildings. The
courtyard may also have had a well
but the area has never been excavated.
On leaving the shop and visitor centre,
housed in a former non-conformist
chapel, visitors will find themselves
opposite the south side of the tower
house where the tour of the castle
begins.

Etal's tower house should not be
considered as the keep of a castle
but as a defensible home for a minor
lordling, his family and retainers.
Initially, it was probably provided
with a courtyard bounded by a simple

wooden palisade, or fence. It was
only later that the stone curtain
walls, gatehouse and corner towers
were added to transform Etal into
a small but impressive castle. It is
therefore appropriate that any tour
of the site should begin with what
was both the earliest and most
important unit of the castle.

*A bird's-eye view of the
castle by Terry Ball,
showing the complete
structure as it might have
appeared in its heyday*

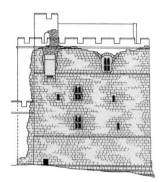

The north elevation of the tower house (the lighter lines show the original form of the building)

A reconstruction drawing of the tower house by Ian Nelson, showing what it might have looked like before the licence to fortify was granted (the lighter lines show the final form of the building)

THE TOWER HOUSE

The first three storeys of the tower house, built in regular courses of large squared stones, appear to be of an earlier date than the uppermost storey and it is probable that they were built before the licence to fortify the house was obtained in 1341. If this is the case, the licence enabled Sir Robert Manners to transform his house into a fully fledged tower house by adding another storey and crenellations, as shown in the reconstruction drawing (below left).

There is also evidence that an entrance to the basement formerly existed in the south wall of the building. Inspection of the external wall at ground-floor level clearly reveals where it was built up with smaller stones when the doorway was removed. Recent investigation of the window embrasure at first-floor level (later converted into an entrance reached by an external wooden stair) found that it was equipped with a *meurtrière*, or murder hole, in its floor through which missiles could be dropped on intruders attempting to break into the building. The doorway which this *meurtrière* protected is depicted in the reconstruction drawing.

The ground floor

The tower house was rectangular in plan with a projecting forebuilding, now collapsed, at its eastern end which housed the main entrance to the tower and the spiral staircase leading to the upper storeys and parapets. *Walk round the side of the tower house towards the entrance to the basement.* The entrance doorway was protected by a drawbar, the cavities for which may be seen on either side of the doorway, just by the steps. In the passageway behind, vertical channels in the walls indicate that the entrance was also protected by a portcullis which would have been lowered from a chamber at first-floor level.

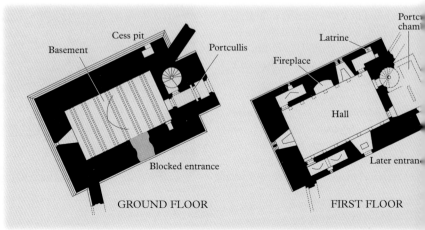

GROUND FLOOR

FIRST FLOOR

Basement

Cess pit

Portcullis

Blocked entrance

Latrine

Portc... cham...

Fireplace

Hall

Later entran...

Beyond the portcullis, the passageway leads to two doorways. The one on the right led to the spiral staircase, of which only a few steps remain (though the projecting fragments clearly indicate its spiral course up to the doorways on each floor), while the one straight ahead led to the basement of the tower. *Walk down the steps into the tower house.* The basement was lit by only one small window and was once roofed by a low-pitched vault supported by seven ribs. Although the vault has now collapsed, its seating at each end and the springing stones of most of its ribs survive, so it is easy to visualise its appearance.

Stone vaults were essential in buildings constructed for defence as they prevented besiegers from breaking into the lower storey and dislodging defenders in the upper storeys by fire. The vault was not overfilled with rubble and mortar, which was the usual method of construction, possibly because the weight of such

an overfill might have been considered too great for such a shallow arched vault to support. The only other feature is a locker or cupboard near the entrance where a lamp would have been stored – essential in such a gloomy room. The basement would have been used to house all the stores needed for the household to survive and, additionally, in times of trouble, their most valuable livestock such as horses and cows. It is now impossible to ascend to the upper storeys but the main features of each floor can be seen from the roofless basement.

The first floor

The main apartment on the first floor was reached from the spiral staircase in the forebuilding. The sockets for the heavy joists which supported its floor may still be seen in the south and north walls. The apartment was very well appointed and was obviously the principal room of the tower house. This would

The tower house, showing the west and south faces, the added uppermost storey and the remains of the curtain wall

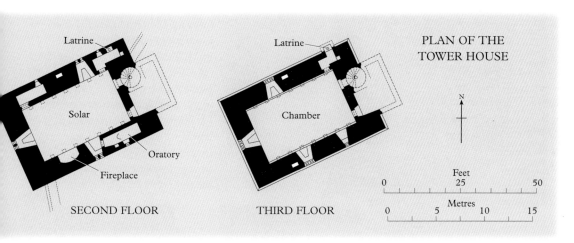

Latrine

Solar

Oratory

Fireplace

SECOND FLOOR

Latrine

Chamber

THIRD FLOOR

PLAN OF THE TOWER HOUSE

N

Feet		
0	25	50

Metres		
0	5	10	15

A cutaway reconstruction drawing of the tower house by Terry Ball

have been where the Manners family took their meals with their guests, companions and retainers, and where business was conducted. It would have been a noisy and bustling place, at the centre of this predominantly male household.

The hall was originally lit by three fine double windows fitted with window seats, the remains of which are visible in the north, south and west walls. At some stage, the window embrasure in the south wall, already mentioned as containing a *meurtrière*, was altered to form an entrance, reached from the courtyard by an external wooden staircase. Obviously, such an entrance was more convenient, particularly for receiving guests, and saved having to negotiate the main entrance and spiral staircase. The defence of the tower would not have been compromised as the external staircase would have been removed in times of danger.

A wide fireplace with an arched lintel is set in the north wall, and the room is provided with three vaulted chambers in the thickness of the walls. The one on the south side of the room is lit by a single window and was plainly a private chamber for some senior household officer, as its doorway was secured on the inside. A chamber to the left of the fireplace, also fitted with a window, probably served as a secure store for more valuable goods while the one in the north-east corner housed a latrine with an internal shaft descending to a cess pit at the foot of the north wall. Finally, a doorway to the right of the entrance from the

spiral staircase led to a chamber in the forebuilding, where a sentry would have been posted to drop the portcullis and alert the occupants of the hall at the first sign of danger.

The walls of the hall would have been plastered and painted with brightly coloured scenes and motifs, and the ceiling and its beams would have been similarly embellished. The hall may also have been decorated with wall-hangings. Heavy and serviceable trestle tables and benches, perhaps a high-backed chair or two for the lord and his lady and various chests, dressers and cupboards would have completed the furnishings of this fine apartment. The reconstruction drawing opposite gives an idea of what the tower house would have looked like in its heyday.

The second floor

The main apartment on the second floor was equally well appointed and was, undoubtedly, the private suite of the Manners family, serving as a withdrawing room by day, enabling the family, particularly the women, to retire from the noisy company of the men in the hall below. At night, it would have served as a bedchamber for the family, affording them the privacy which their status demanded. It would have been furnished accordingly with a great curtained bed, a number of truckle beds, chairs, stools, chests and closets and would have been painted and decorated in the same way as the hall.

The apartment was lit by three mullioned windows with window seats, as in the hall below but in the south facing window, the seating on the left of the embrasure was omitted to allow for a doorway into a chamber in the thickness of the wall, lit by a window with an ornamented head. Although it is not really visible from the basement of the tower house, the floor at the eastern end shows signs of having had some structure built upon it, and a recess in the wall near the entrance may have housed a piscina. It is therefore probable that this chamber served as a private oratory with an altar at its eastern end. Significantly, an identical arrangement exists on the same floor of Chipchase Tower in Northumberland.

The room was provided with two further mural chambers. The one in the north-west corner of the room, lit by a small window, might have served as a strong room for the family's valuables and money, while the other, in the north-east corner, contained a latrine above the one serving the hall, with an internal shaft joining the same cess pit. Finally, a further door led into a chamber in the fore-building which might have been used as a wardrobe or dressing room or, alternatively, as a retiring room for waiting maids where they would have been close at hand when called upon to attend their mistress.

The ground floor of the tower house, showing the vault seating and the springing stones of its ribs

The first-floor fireplace in the tower house

The south window embrasure in the second-floor apartment of the tower house, showing the doorway in the thickness of the embrasure leading to the oratory

The north-east corner of the interior of the tower house, showing the joist sockets of the upper floors, the first-floor window embrasure with window seats and a doorway to a latrine

The third floor

Look up at the topmost storey. The third-floor apartment, as has already been suggested, was probably added after the licence to fortify the house was obtained. It is lit by four windows, three of which are mullioned windows with window seats like those below. It was also fitted with a latrine in a mural chamber above those of the floors below. However, in this case, the entrance differs in that it has a flat lintel instead of the arch used elsewhere in the tower. In addition, the latrine was situated in a housing projecting from the exterior wall and equipped with an external chute. The housing and corbelling which supported it has now collapsed but if you go out of the tower house and look up at the wall outside you can see a large scar near the top which clearly shows where it was. The fact that the latrine differed in this way supports the case for the later addition of this storey, as it would have been very difficult to break through the solid walls of the lower floors to join up with the latrine shafts below.

The apartment is not fitted with a fireplace or any mural chambers; it seems that this storey was built to a more basic plan with less thought for the comfort of its occupants. It may be that it served as a dormitory or barrack room for a garrison of military retainers. This would make sense, as sentries on duty, or a garrison in time of alarm, would have been ideally placed to man the top of the tower quickly. If this was the case, the additional chamber in the forebuilding could well have served as a private chamber for their commanding officer.

The parapets

Look up at the roof as you come out of the tower house. Nothing much remains of the roof or the parapets of the tower, and it is only possible to guess at their appearance. It is probable that the roof was steeply pitched and had stone gable ends as was usual in border towers. The parapets would have been crenellated and might have been equipped with corner turrets, though no evidence for this exists. A tall turret above the spiral staircase certainly did exist, as part of its vault above roof level may still be seen. Its elevation would have made it an ideal look-out post for a sentry.

THE GATEHOUSE

Walk across the courtyard to the gatehouse, the second major unit of the castle. It shows a considerable degree of sophistication both in terms of its architecture and its defences. It post-dates the tower house by a number of years but must have been completed, together with the curtain walls and corner towers, before 1368 when Etal was recorded as a castle. The gatehouse is two storeys in height but the flanking towers on either side of the gateway were carried up a further storey.

The entrance, always the most vulnerable part of a castle's defences, was very well protected. Although there was never a ditch surrounding the castle to protect the walls, there might have been a pit in front of the gatehouse for a drawbridge, as there are slots for cables above the front of the gateway. Pivoting just within the gateway approach, it could have been winched into an upright position to block the entrance recess completely. Sockets show that stout drawbars would have been drawn across its rear which would have enabled it to withstand battering rams.

In addition, this effective barrier was protected by a roofed, timber fighting gallery extending across and projecting in front of the flanking towers. This gallery was supported on corbelled brackets on each flanking tower, the remains of which may still be seen on the front of the gatehouse. It was accessed by a doorway at first-floor level in the north flanking tower. Defenders in the fighting gallery would have been in an excellent position to harass assailants attempting to attack the drawbridge.

Even if attackers succeeded in breaking through these defences, they would still have been confronted with both the strong iron-strapped timber portcullis and the sturdy iron-studded timber main gates, and would have been faced by a withering fire from the wall tops above and the gallery behind.

East elevation of the gatehouse (the lighter lines show the original form of the building)

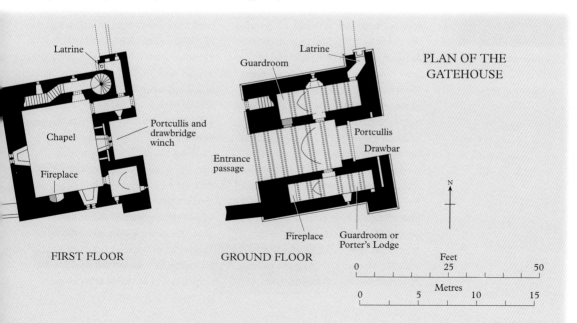

PLAN OF THE GATEHOUSE

FIRST FLOOR

Latrine

Chapel

Fireplace

Portcullis and drawbridge winch

GROUND FLOOR

Guardroom

Latrine

Entrance passage

Portcullis

Drawbar

Fireplace

Guardroom or Porter's Lodge

N

Feet
0   25   50

Metres
0   5   10   15

The interior of the entrance passage, showing the remains of the vault and its supporting ribs

The guardroom to the north of the entrance passage

The ground floor

The interior of the gatehouse can now only be reached from the courtyard, as the modern portcullis is kept shut. The wide entrance passage was formerly roofed by a high arched vault supported on six ribs. Two of the ribs still exist, supporting the rear wall of the gatehouse, but the others, together with the vault, have collapsed. As in the tower house, the vault was not overfilled which, once the roof above perished, would have hastened its disintegration by exposure to the elements.

On either side of the entrance passage, doorways led to guardrooms with arched and ribbed vaults. The chamber on the right is lit by a small window so high in the wall that it interrupts the vaulting. It also has a recess for a lamp and a wide fireplace at its western end. It is easy to imagine the gatekeeper and guards crouched in front of their fire to keep warm on their long spells of night duty. The chamber on the left of the entrance passage was also lit by a small window but, at some stage, the stonework beneath the window has been robbed out to form a crude fireplace using the window as a flue. The chamber was also equipped with a latrine built into the thickness of the wall. It had a projecting housing, now collapsed, and an external chute. A second doorway, which has now been blocked up, once led back to the entrance passage. It appears to be a later insertion.

The first floor

Go back out of the guard chamber and look at the back of the gatehouse. The first floor was reached by a doorway in the rear wall. The door was protected by a drawbar, and led to the first floor via a steep flight of steps, a few of which remain. Because the floor of the main apartment has perished, access to the stairway has been sealed but details of the first floor can be seen from the roofless entrance passage. From the landing, a doorway led into a particularly handsome apartment, lit by three traceried windows fitted with window seats. Slots on either side of the eastern window above the gate were for the cables which operated the drawbridge and portcullis. The apartment is fitted with an arched fireplace, which at some stage has been reduced to half its width by blocking up its right-hand side. In the south-east corner, a doorway led into a small vaulted chamber lit by two windows, while in the north-east corner, a passage led to the fighting gallery and to a latrine in a projecting housing in the rear of the north flanking tower. Windows in this passage overlook the gateway recess and the east curtain wall.

The first floor was, therefore, primarily devoted to the military function of the gatehouse and was central to the defence of the castle. However, it was not unusual for the upper floors of gatehouses to serve a dual purpose. Castles were rarely under permanent threat of attack and although vigilance could never be relaxed so near to the violent Scottish border, daily life within the castle was relatively secure. In many castles, the upper floors were used as living quarters. Indeed, at Bywell, Bothal and Dunstanburgh, all in Northumberland, the principal living quarters are in the gatehouses.

At Etal, the ornate traceried windows of the first-floor apartment suggest that it may have been designed to serve as the castle's chapel. Another similar example exists in the Umfraville stronghold at Prudhoe in Northumberland where, in the thirteenth century, the first floor of the gatehouse was converted into a chapel with an altar placed in a projecting oriel bay at its east end.

In Etal's case, a moveable altar must have been placed in front of the windlass gear which was probably concealed by a low carved screen or curtain when the chapel was in use.

The upperworks

A spiral staircase on the first-floor landing ascended within the north flanking tower to the roof of the gatehouse. Little remains of the staircase or the northern tower, which originally rose to the same height as the south flanking tower. The remains of a small, rib-vaulted chamber in the south flanking tower may still be seen. It would have sheltered the sentries on duty. With the exception of slight traces of a projecting turret at the rear of the gatehouse, the parapets have all perished, but the reconstruction drawing gives an

The east interior wall of the gatehouse, showing one of the traceried windows with the slots for the cables of the portcullis and the drawbridge (NB: the present portcullis is modern)

The rear of the gatehouse, showing the entrance passage, the door to the first floor and the projecting rear turret; on the side are the scars left by the collapse of the two latrine housings

The south wall of the south-west corner tower, showing the corbels which supported an overhanging latrine

A cutaway reconstruction drawing of the gatehouse by Terry Ball

impression of what the building would have looked like when it was complete.

THE SOUTH-WEST TOWER

Two of the vulnerable angles of the roughly rectangular curtain wall were protected by the tower house and the gatehouse. The third angle, in the south-east, was also protected by a small tower, now attached to the custodian's house. If you go through the doorway in its east wall, you will see that the ground-floor chamber of the tower is roofed by a vault supported by three ribs. The crown of

the vault is no less than four metres above the floor and its disproportionate height is explained by two sets of corbels on the sides of the vault. These show that the chamber was once fitted with a loft, reached by a ladder – an effective way of doubling the storage space available.

The chamber was equipped with two lockers, and was originally lit by a window in its west wall. However, after the adjoining house was built, a doorway was forced through the window embrasure into the tower so only traces of its truncated sill remain. The vault was overfilled, which accounts for its survival, but little remains of the tower's upper floor. It must have been reached by an external staircase or, alternatively, from the parapet walk of the adjoining curtain wall. The only clue to the internal arrangements of the first floor are two projecting double corbels on the exterior of the south wall, which indicate that it was equipped with an overhanging latrine.

POSSIBLE SITE OF A NORTH-EAST TOWER

It seems highly unlikely that the fourth corner of the curtain wall was unprotected but, so far, no trace of a tower has been found. A geophysical survey conducted in 1988 recorded a large area of high density just below the north-east corner of the curtain wall, which might be associated with

the tumbled debris of a fallen tower but only future excavation will establish whether such a tower existed.

THE CURTAIN WALL

The curtain wall, the course of which is shown on the plan of the castle, has only survived to any height between the gatehouse and the south-west tower. Further short lengths may be seen on two sides of the tower house. The original height of the curtain wall can be seen in the tower's south face. The visible remains of the wall show that it was not particularly strong, being only 1.7 metres thick on the north and west sides of the courtyard and a mere metre thick on the south side, which meant that corbels had to be built along the top of its interior face to make a wide enough wall walk for defenders to man. It is clear that the walls were never intended to be proof against a major assault, but rather were built to give protection against lightly armed raiding parties who were a constant threat on the border.

THE COURTYARD

In medieval times, the courtyard would have been filled with buildings, some freestanding and others built against the curtain walls. Blocked apertures and disturbed stonework in the surviving south

curtain wall are a clear indication that buildings were erected against the wall, and excavations in 1983 found traces of ovens near the tower house, so it is probable that the castle's kitchens were built against the north wall. Castles had to be self-sufficient, so the courtyard would have contained kitchens, a bake-house, brewery, laundry, smithy, stabling and residential quarters, as well as all the buildings necessary for managing a manorial estate. The reconstruction drawing on page three gives an idea of what this small but impressive stronghold looked like. It was once a secure and bustling home for its proud and knightly owners, their family and a whole community of military retainers, household and estate officers, servants and craftsmen, and it was also, in times of danger, the refuge of the population of the nearby village.

Part of the south curtain wall, showing projecting corbels which supported the parapet walk and a blocked-up feature indicating that a building was erected against the wall

The south-west corner tower, showing the entrance and the surviving south curtain wall

HISTORY

❖

WHEN THE NORMANS invaded England in 1066, they speedily established their rule over southern England but the fiercely independent spirit of the mixed Saxon and Danish population of the North and the antagonism of the neighbouring Scots made the task of subjugating the North both difficult and protracted. It was not until the end of the century that the border with Scotland was firmly established on the Tweed–Solway line, and the north of England was brought under Norman control. Only then, in 1100, was Henry I able to embark on the colonisation of Northumberland, securing the county by creating a series of baronies between the Tweed and the Tyne and granting them to Normans of proven loyalty and valour. These baronies were held directly from the king in return for military service, each being assessed in value according to the number of knights it could be expected to supply in times of war or campaigning.

To protect their holdings on an insecure frontier, these newly created barons promptly set about the erection of earth and timber castles to serve as strongholds and administrative centres. There, they could maintain themselves and their followers in relative security and carry out their duties as local representatives of the king. The castles of Morpeth, Alnwick, Bolam, Mitford, Prudhoe, Wark and Wooler all date from this time of rapid colonization and formed the nuclei of the northern baronies set up by Henry I.

Etal was a small manorial holding within the barony of Wooler. The barony was granted to Robert Muschamp and was valued at four knights' service. It stretched from the North Sea to the Cheviot Hills and was only a few kilometres from the Scottish border. As it straddled all possible invasion routes from Scotland into eastern England, it is clear that Robert would need to protect his holding.

Robert Muschamp would have arrived in his barony with a sufficient force to establish himself securely in his newly acquired land. The core of this force would have been a number of Norman knights who served him in accordance with the terms of his feudal obligations to the king. These superior retainers would, initially, have formed an integral part of Muschamp's household, acting as military officers, bodyguards and companions. However, once the barony was firmly established, these knights became sub-tenants, holding land within the barony in return for continuing feudal service.

THE MANNERS FAMILY OF ETAL

Although no record exists revealing the identity of the knights who accompanied the Muschamps to Wooler, a document of 1180 shows that a Robert Manners was already holding lands worth half a knight's service within the barony. There can be little doubt that this grant had been made as a result of valuable service rendered by Robert and his forebears. Similarly, it is highly probable that the land Robert held was the manor of Etal, as a document of 1232

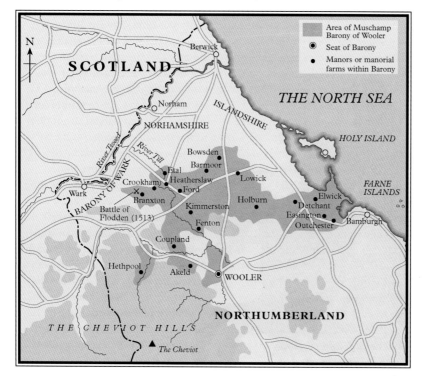

Map of the Muschamp barony of Wooler, c.1200

records a boundary dispute between another Robert Manners of Etal and William Muschamp of Barmoor. This second Robert appears again in a list of sub-tenants within the barony, compiled in 1250, where he is listed as holding the manor of Etal for half a knight's service.

These early generations of the Manners family would have lived in a sturdy timber hall complex within a palisaded enclosure. However, Etal's proximity to the troubled Scottish border would have spurred the family to replace their timber hall with a stronger building in stone as soon as was practicable. No evidence exists to date the erection of such a structure, but it might have been built in the final years of the thirteenth century when a third Robert was recorded as lord of Etal. He is first mentioned in 1274 and was knighted in 1278 for his services to the king. Sir Robert must have been a notable figure on the border and his house both secure and well appointed, as in 1291 the Archbishop of York chose to stay at Etal in preference to neighbouring Ford while on a visit to the North. Shortly after this visit, in 1296, Robert's lands were valued at the substantial sum of £27 10s 6d. Sir Robert must have seen a lifetime of service in the Scottish wars during the reigns of both Edward I and Edward II. The date of his death is unknown but his son, another Robert, is recorded as lord of Etal in 1336.

By this time, Edward III was actively pursuing his grandfather's ambition to subjugate Scotland and it is probable that this Robert, like his father, gained his knighthood for his service in this new round of wars. The position throughout the border region was still desperate, as the Scots, unable to face the full might of Edward's armies in the field, seized every opportunity of surprise attack and fought back with devastating raids over the English border. This was a time when land-holders were encouraged to fortify their homes or erect new defences to protect themselves against Scottish raiders. Every man of substance built what he could afford, some merely building a fighting top to their houses, others adding a sturdy self-contained tower to their

Sir Robert Manners, Lord of Etal, c.1270, artist's impression by Ian Nelson

homes and the more affluent erecting minor castles to protect their lands.

In 1338 the Manners' neighbours, the Herons of Ford, obtained a licence to fortify their home and changed their manor house into a walled castle. In 1341 Robert Manners followed suit, gaining a licence to fortify his house at Etal. The lower three storeys of the existing tower house may well have been built before 1341, as there are distinct signs that the uppermost storey and the parapets were added later. This would suggest that the licence was obtained to transform an existing structure into the fine tower house we see today. It would appear that the rest of the castle was built later still, and that the tower house was originally conceived as an independent structure set within a palisaded courtyard, as a survey of border fortifications, compiled in 1355, refers to Etal as a 'fortalice', a term used to describe a building of lesser strength than a castle. Building work might have been delayed by the death of Robert in 1354.

Robert Manners was succeeded by his son, John, who must have been responsible for the rest of the castle as we know it today. The curtain walls, towers and gatehouse must have been completed before 1368 when, in another survey, Etal was recorded as a castle. John died before 1402, when it is known that his son, another Robert, was lord of Etal. This Robert may have married a Baxter heiress, as their lands in Lanton, Kirknewton, Pawston, Coupland, Milfield and Crookhouse were, by this date, in the hands of the Manners family.

Robert Manners was followed by his son, John, who is chiefly known for his part in a disastrous feud between the Manners and the Herons of Ford. The cause of the feud is unclear, but it would appear that a tangled web of feudal rights and a power struggle for pre-eminence may have been at the heart of the disagreement. The feud culminated in 1428 when William Heron, the son and heir of the lord of Ford, was killed with one of his followers. Before matters got further out of hand, a commission was set up to investigate William's death. His widow claimed that her husband had been 'maliciously slayne' by John Manners but John stoutly defended himself, claiming that William had come to Etal with an armed force and had led 'a gret assaut in shotying of arrowes and strykying with swerdes'. In the ensuing mêlée, William was killed but the 'innocent' John was more than a spear's length away at the time. However, he seems to have ended his defence on a more contrite note, for the commissioners reported that 'the sayd John all tymes sore has repented'. They appear to have arrived at a compromise judgement which called upon John to give

View of the tower house from the west with the gatehouse beyond

worth only a twentieth of a knight's service instead of the original assessment of a half. There is little doubt that the continuing border strife was a major factor in this state of affairs but as Ford Castle and its estate suffered a similar drop in value it is likely that the bitter feud had contributed to this particular local decline.

Robert Manners, however, was an active leader who accompanied Sir Henry Percy on his duties on the border. He was awarded a knighthood for his services and, furthermore, was granted the goods and rents of the outlawed Sir Robert Ogle. Thus, he was able to restore his family fortunes. He was killed during the Wars of the Roses when, serving with the Percys in the Lancastrian cause, both he and the Earl of Northumberland fell at the Battle of Towton in 1461.

Sir Robert was succeeded by his son, another Robert, who was also knighted for his services on the Scottish border. He married the sister and heiress of Lord Roos, and Robert's son, George, who succeeded his father in 1495, inherited the Roos barony and lands from his mother. George further advanced his family's position by marrying the niece of the late King Edward IV, allying himself with some of the highest families in the land. He abandoned Etal, preferring a less troubled existence on estates he had inherited in Rutland, leaving his ancestral home in the hands of a constable, John

William's widow 250 marks and, in addition, pay for 500 masses to be said for William's soul.

Protests and recriminations rumbled on, with the Herons being supported by the powerful Umfraville family and the Manners by the Ogles, Middletons and Lilburns. The feud figured in a series of law suits and, in all probability, in less lawful actions, as an extraordinary number of leading local personages, including John and his eldest son, appear to have died before the ruinous feud ended in 1438.

John died in that year and was succeeded by his second son, Robert, who found that his patrimony had severely fallen in value. Etal Castle was in ruins, its lands were valued at between a penny and two pence an acre and its cottages in the township worth only two pence a year in rent. The whole estate was held to be

Collingwood, who was provided with a small garrison to defend the castle.

It was during John Collingwood's time as constable that Etal was suddenly thrust into the forefront of national events. In 1513, an army of 30,000 Scots led by James IV invaded England while Henry VIII and a powerful English army were fighting in France. The major castles of Wark and Norham were bombarded and subsequently fell to the Scots who then moved on to Etal and Ford. Neither castle had been built to withstand a major siege, and after a brief bombardment, Etal was captured and garrisoned by the Scots. Ford quickly followed and became James's headquarters while the Scottish army encamped on Flodden Hill to await the English response. That response was swift and decisive. The Earl of Surrey, with a hastily levied army of 20,000 northerners, outmanoeuvred the Scots and in a bitterly fought battle inflicted a crushing defeat on the invaders. James and nearly all of his nobles

Reconstruction drawing of the Battle of Flodden, 1513, by Ivan Lapper

The James Tower, Ford Castle, where James IV is alleged to have stayed before the Battle of Flodden

and commanders were killed and James's formidable train of artillery was hauled to Etal for safekeeping.

George Manners, Lord Roos, died in 1514, leaving his son, Thomas, as heir to his title and properties. Like his father, Thomas chose to live in the South, and Etal remained in the hands of John Collingwood as constable. In 1516 and 1517, Lord Dacre frequently stayed at Etal, using it as one of his bases while attending to his duties as deputy captain of Norham Castle on the border. By 1535 John had been succeeded as constable by Henry Collingwood, who was reported by the Lord Warden of the East Marches as being 'a sharp borderer keeping a good house', and in command of a troop of thirty horsemen.

In a survey of 1541, however, it is plain that Etal was paying the price of disinterested ownership, as the castle was reported by royal commissioners as being 'for lack of reparacons in very grete decaye and many necessary houses within the same become ruynous and fallen to the ground'. The commissioners urged its immediate repair, not only because of the protection it afforded to the local inhabitants but because of the base it provided 'for the conveying of ordenance and armyes into Scotland'. It might have been this report which persuaded the Crown to commence negotiations to transfer Etal to royal ownership, as in 1547,

Thomas Manners, then Earl of Rutland, finally severed the Manners' connection with the North by ceding Etal and all of their northern possessions to the Crown in exchange for lands elsewhere.

ROYAL AND LATER OCCUPANCY

In 1549 the castle is mentioned again when Sir John Ellerker, a royal officer, was recorded as being in command of 100 horsemen and 200 foot-soldiers there. Apparently, a force of this size was considered too large a responsibility for the Collingwoods to command, though it appears that they retained their position as constables or bailiffs under the Crown. In 1564, in Elizabeth I's reign, the Marquis of Winchester visited the castle. It is evident that the advice of the earlier commission had been ignored as the Marquis declared that 'the Queen's house at Etal is greatly decayed, scant able to lodge the captain'. Again, in 1584, commissioners reported Etal as 'decaied for want of reparacion of longe contynuance', and urged the expenditure of £200 to restore it to its former strength.

The union of the English and Scottish crowns in 1603 ended Etal's active role in history and with it any likelihood of the border commissioners' recommendations being carried out. The need for the Crown to hold castles at strategic points on the border ceased, and in 1604 the manor of Etal was surveyed with a view to granting it to a new tenant. It was found to comprise 4971 acres of land, of which only 1984 acres lay in Etal itself, for the term 'manor' included all the lands which had formerly been held by the Manners family in Bowsden, Humbleton, Kilham, Howtel, Hetherslaw, Ewart, Berrington, Buckton, Goswick and Norham. The Crown granted the manor to George Hume, recently created Baron Hume of Berwick for an annual payment of £48 6s 8d. In 1611, Baron Hume died and Etal became the property of Lord Howard de Walden, Earl of Suffolk. In 1636, the Earl sold the tenancy to Robert Carr for £2400.

Robert Carr was a Scot, related to the Carrs who had succeeded the Herons as owners of Ford Castle. He enjoyed a rather chequered career. When the Scots invaded England to support the Parliamentarians in the Civil War against Charles I, Robert joined his fellow countrymen and fought actively for Parliament. He then had a change of heart and, after note-worthy efforts for the Royalist cause, was awarded a payment of £400 and created a baronet. Robert's previous allies were incensed by his change of allegiance so when Charles I was captured and beheaded, Robert could hardly have been surprised when his estate was promptly forfeited by Parliament. In 1660, however, when the Stuart dynasty was restored, Sir Robert was able to reclaim his lands, though he proved to be such a bad manager that he accumulated debts totalling £6000. He handed the estate over to his son, William, in 1661 and emigrated to New England. He must have fared no better there either for in 1667 he died in Bristol on his way back to Etal.

Sir William Carr proved a more stable character and spent much of his energies in legal disputes to establish clearly defined boundaries between himself and his neighbours, possibly a matter still outstanding since the feud with the Herons over 200 years before. The castle and estate remained in the hands of the Carr family until the reign of George III, by which time the castle

The tower house of Belsay Castle, built by the Middleton family, was remodelled to form part of a new mansion

was no longer the residence of the family. The changed state of the border since the Act of Union enabled landholders to concentrate on the development of their estates and accumulate wealth instead of merely eking out a living from war-torn lands. Their newly found security and increasing prosperity caused many border castles and towers to be abandoned in favour of newly built, more comfortable residences. Other stark, defensive buildings were remodelled and turned into a wing of a new mansion such as at Belsay or were converted into stately homes such as the castles of Alnwick, Ford and Chillingham.

The first Lord Joicey who purchased the Etal estate in 1908

Etal Castle, like Belsay, was eventually abandoned in favour of a handsome and comfortable manor house built in 1748 at the other end of the village. Time and weather were allowed to take a greater toll on the old home of the Manners family than the Scots had ever done. From the Carrs, Etal passed by female descent to a number of connected families. The last descendants of the Carrs to own and live in Etal were Lord Frederick and Lady Augusta Fitzclarence. Lord Frederick, an illegitimate son of William IV, did much to tidy up the ruined castle and placed in front of the gatehouse a pair of naval cannon salvaged from the wreck of the Royal George. Lady Augusta died in 1876 and the estate was sold to James Laing, a shipbuilder from Sunderland. In 1908, the Laing family sold the castle to the first Lord Joicey who had also purchased the neighbouring estate of Ford. It seems somehow fitting that the estates of those bitter rivals, the Manners and the Herons, should now be peacefully united under the ownership of one family. The appearance of Etal village now owes much to the careful management of the Joicey family. The well-kept cottages with their neat and colourful gardens, the charming old inn, recently faithfully restored to its original appearance after a fire, and the secluded manor house all delight the visitor. Above all, the conservation of the castle initiated by the Joicey family and now continued by English Heritage has ensured that future generations will have the opportunity to undertand what life was like on the border in harsher and less hospitable times, and to learn more about the events which shaped this region.

❖ GLOSSARY ❖

Traces of these architectural features can be found at Etal Castle

Bratische or overhung fighting gallery

An overhanging timber structure which was erected on wall tops or wall faces and enabled defenders to harass assailants from apertures in its floor and walls. Such a gallery once existed on the front of the gatehouse.

Chamfered rebate

A point where the walls are set back in plan from those below, eg. on the exterior of the tower house.

Corbels and double corbels

Projecting stones firmly seated in a wall to support beams or over-hanging structures, eg. the latrine housings on the exterior of the gatehouse and south-west tower; and supports for the fighting gallery on the outside of the gatehouse.

Crenellations

A parapet wall protecting defenders, pierced at intervals to enable them to fire at attacking forces. A licence had to be obtained from the Crown before building such defences.

Doorway with arched head and chamfered surrounds

A doorway where the stonework of the surround has been decoratively rounded, or chamfered, indicating that the door was fitted on the far side of the doorway, eg. the entrances to the latrines in the tower house.

Doorway with arched head and rebated surrounds

A doorway where the stonework of the surround has been cut back to allow for a door which opened on the near side of the doorway, eg. the entrances from the spiral staircase in the tower house.

Doorway with flat lintel

A doorway with a flat top, generally fitted where low roofs prevented the fitting of an arched head, eg. the door-way to the oratory in the tower house which was situated inside a window embrasure.

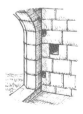

Drawbar sockets

A hole for a heavy beam of timber which could be drawn across the rear of the door to give added strength against forcing, eg. in the entrance recess of the gatehouse; and the entrance to the tower house.

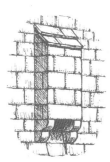

Overhung latrine housing with an external chute

A latrine built out over an external wall with a protective housing supported on corbels and an external chute discharging to the ground on the exterior of the building. Like parapets, these housings were relatively flimsy structures and at Etal, all have now collapsed, although traces of them are still visible, eg. on the top storey of the tower house; the ground and top storeys of the gatehouse; and the south-west tower.

Projecting chamfered base courses

The enlarged footing or plinth of a building, eg. on the tower house, gatehouse and south-west tower.

Ribbed vault

A ceiling supported by a double chamfered beam or rib. All the major vaults at Etal were of this type of construction.

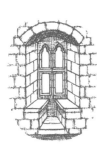

Splayed window embrasure with an arched head

A hole for a window which widens towards the interior of the room to admit more light. The embrasure depicted is fitted with chamfered window seats and the window is rebated to take shutters, eg. on the upper floors of the tower house.

Window with ogee head and chamfered surrounds

A window shouldered at its head, eg. on the uppermost storeys of the tower house.

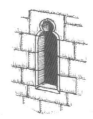

Window with cusped ogee head and chamfered surrounds

A window in which the shoulders of the ogee head are extended inwards to form projecting points, eg. the window of the oratory on the second floor of the tower house.

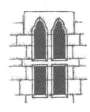

Window with double lights, transoms, ogee heads and chamfered surrounds

A window divided into two by a vertical mullion and each of the two lights thus formed being further divided by horizontal transoms. The upper sections are fitted with ogee heads and the surrounds are chamfered, eg. on the upper floors of the tower house.

Window with double lights and traceried head

A window with a highly decorative sculpted head generally fitted in buildings of particular importance such as halls, withdrawing rooms and those designed for religious use, eg. on the first floor of the gatehouse.